It's OK to write in this book!

This book belongs to...

Am I Supposed to Feel This Way?

A Seven-Year-Old Birth Child's
Experiences of Adoption

Elizabeth Archer

WORDCATCHER publishing

Am I Supposed to Feel This Way?

A Seven-Year-Old Birth Child's Experiences of Adoption

© 2016 Elizabeth Archer
Illustrations © Martine Cucciniello

British Library Cataloguing in Publication Data.
A catalogue record for this book is available from the British Library.

Published by Onion Custard Kids, an imprint of Wordcatcher Publishing, Cardiff, UK.

Paperback format: ISBN: 9781912056293
First Edition: June, 2017

Contents

My Name is Oliver

Hi! My name is Oliver and I am

seven years old.

I live with Mum and Dad,

and my little brother Max,

who we have adopted.

When I was younger all I wanted was a little brother or sister.
All my friends seemed to have a brother or sister to play with, and I wanted to be just like them too.

Mum and Dad told me that they couldn't have any more babies after me and that made me sad.

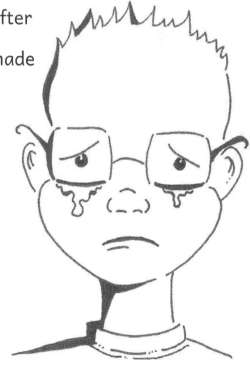

I didn't really understand why.

Are your parents talking about adopting a brother or sister for you too?

How does this make you feel?

(draw your expression whenever you see an empty circle like this!)

If they are, you're very lucky and very special.

But it will be hard at times.

Sometimes, even now, I don't want my brother to play with my toys and I don't want him to spend time with Mum and Dad.

4

Sometimes I even still wish it was just me, but these feelings go away and I am really happy that Mum and Dad found a brother for me.

He is just right for all our family.

My friends at school who have brothers and sisters say the same things. Sometimes they also wish they didn't have them around.

So now I think it must be quite normal to feel this way.

What is Adoption?

Mum told me that sometimes mums and dads aren't able to care for their own children, even though they love them very much.

Sometimes they are unable to keep them safe and protect them as we all need our parents to. Then it is thought best by a Judge, (one of those people who wears a gown and a wig in a Law Court), that these children need to be cared for by another family that will love them, no matter what.

Children can be adopted at different ages. Most children who are adopted have experienced some difficulties in their young lives.

They may have been left alone and not cuddled as we have. They may not have had someone to cook them tasty and healthy meals.

They may not have had nice new

toys bought for them at Christmas

time or on their birthday. In fact,

sometimes their birthdays

are even forgotten...

Think how that must feel.

How would you feel if your family forgot your birthday?

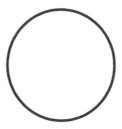

Imagine how sad, confused, and alone they must have felt at times.

Try to remember when you feel sad,

confused or lonely that your little

brother or sister may have

felt like that too.

Think of times when you have felt

sad, lonely, or confused. Can you

remember why you felt like this?

But you are lucky, as you have a fantastic family to help you cope with all your feelings and as a family, you can learn to help your brother or sister with their feelings too.

Family

The Start of My Story

Let me tell you my story.

One day, when I was 5 years old, Mum, Dad, and I sat and watched a film together. It was called Stuart Little and was all about a couple who adopted a clever little talking mouse as their son.

After the film was over they told me their news – they were also looking to adopt a little girl or a little boy.

WOW!! I jumped around with excitement. Mum and Dad even let me jump on the sofa – I was so happy!

But when was my new brother or sister coming to live with us?

?

Mum and Dad told me that they had to be approved as Adopters first.

An Adopter is someone who has been approved to permanently look after another person's child. It might be when a Judge in a Court has agreed that the child's own family are not able to care for them properly and keep them safe.

An Adopter will raise the child as if they were their own.

14

They had to go to panel and sit in front of lots of people – Social Workers and Managers, other adopters and sometimes grown-ups who were adopted themselves when they were children.

They are all people who know about adoption.

Then they make the decision, whether this is a family that could adopt a child.

We are going through this, and now we have to show that we can care for a child that has had a difficult start in life.

Now that I knew about our possible new arrival, I met our Social Worker, Christine, who worked with Mum and Dad. She is lovely. I really like talking to her and she is always happy to answer any questions that I have.

I liked being asked about what I wanted and what I thought. I really liked being involved.

What would you like to ask your Social Worker?

Write some of your questions here...

I drew pictures for Christine and she made me feel special.

Mum and Dad bought me a special book, which I chose from the shop myself – it was a Superhero book. It was blank, so I could write down any thoughts or feelings I had about getting a little brother or sister.

They let me write down anything, whether it was good or bad.

I wrote down questions I had as soon as I thought of them, and anything I was worried about.

I even wrote a list of things I would like to do with my new brother or sister.

I wrote that if it was a boy,
I wanted to teach them football,
and headers, and to play with my
building bricks.

If it was a girl, we could play
Knights and Princesses and we
could go on magical adventures
together.

We called this book my

MAYBE BABY book.

I didn't really mind if it was a boy or a girl, or even how old they were. I did NOT want to hear crying at night, or have to deal with STINKY BUMS or

POOEY NAPPIES!

I also didn't want them to break or bite any of my favourite toys.

I spent quite a lot of time writing in my book and I also drew lots of pictures for my new brother or sister.

Sometimes I found it easier to write down how I felt on my own in my book, rather than telling Mum and Dad.

This book was just for me to write in, but I loved being able to share it with Christine, our Social Worker.

Mum and Dad explained that there wasn't a right or a wrong way to feel.

They encouraged me to talk about anything that was troubling me, so we could sort it out together.

What would you call your book?

What would you write in your book?

Can you draw something special to give to your new brother or sister?

Success!

Mum and Dad got approved at the panel meeting with the brilliant support of Christine.

I was REALLY happy!

Mum and Dad bought me a fab new scooter to thank me for all my help!

"Will we get our baby now?" I asked.

24

Not just yet

replied Mum.

Now we have to wait for the Social Workers to find you a little brother or sister that will be just right for our family

explained Dad.

It seemed like ages and Mum and Dad went to several 'Children's Evenings' to find out about children who needed a new home.

We have to wait, Oliver. We need to find the right child for all of us. This is a big decision, and we want to get it right.

Mum said quietly to me,

I waited...

and waited...

and waited...

I waited

and waited some more...

and then...

Dad said
"We think we may have found
your new brother.
He's called Max."

Hooray! Hooray!

At last!

I was so excited.

Max was a little baby, not a boy like me. He was just seven months old.

"When can he come and live with us?"

I asked.

Not just yet

replied Mum.

Now we need to go to the Matching Panel

Dad explained.

This would be like the first panel, but this time they all needed to agree that baby Max could come and live with us.

Oh, no... more waiting!

I sighed.

Would baby Max EVER get here?

Then, eventually,

the time did come!

Meeting Max

First, Mum and Dad went to meet baby Max at the Foster Carer's home.

A Foster Carer is someone whose job it is to look after children who have had to leave their birth families. Sometimes they only stay a short time and then move to live with their 'Forever Families'.

Sometimes they stay longer with their Foster Carers until the right family is found. There are different types of Foster Carers and different reasons why children stay for a short time or a long time.

Some children stay with their Foster Carers until they are grown up.

That made me think a bit.

What must it be like to go from your own family to a foster family, and then go to a new mum and dad?

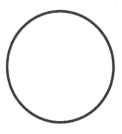

I wanted to be there as well, but I was told I needed to wait a little longer so Mum and Dad could get to know him first. I would meet baby Max a few days later.

A few days later after school,

I went to meet baby Max at the

Foster Carer's home.

It felt funny seeing him. He didn't

do much, but he did giggle when he

went in his door bouncer.

He sat on my lap

and we had

a cuddle.

I really like the Foster Carer's dog.
She jumped up on me and bounced
around the room. She was more fun
than Max!

Mum and Dad took me to get an
ice cream on the way home as a
special treat.

I was very excited about baby Max
coming to our house.

A few days later, baby Max came to spend the day with us.

He cried quite a lot, especially when he was hungry.

He also cried in the car when we were going to and from the Foster Carer's home. I didn't really like being in the back of the car with him as he was VERY loud.

After lots of visits, the big day finally came. We were bringing Max home for good!

Bringing Max Home

I had some time off of school to go with Mum and Dad to pick Max up from the Foster Carer's home.

It was early in the morning, and I felt both nervous, and also excited.

Mum and Dad walked back to school with me at lunchtime with Max in his pushchair.
The ladies in the school office rushed out to see him and made a fuss of him while I was taken back to my classroom.

I hadn't really wanted to go back
to school but I was in the Christmas
play and nobody wanted me
to miss it.

Mum had to stay at home to look
after Max but Dad and Granddad
came to watch me in my play,
which I really enjoyed.

A few days later, Mum came with
me on my school trip to the
Christmas Panto. It was Dad's
turn to stay at home with
Max this time.

The panto was brilliant! I was even asked to go up on stage at the end of the show. I felt very nervous. I had been asked once before when I was with Mum and Grandma and just couldn't do it then.

This time it was different. I felt more confident inside. I thought about Max, and that I was a proud big brother now.

So, I DID IT!

I was very nervous to begin with, but then I found my courage and began to enjoy it. I even made some funny jokes at the end and made everyone laugh!

I was very popular with all my friends and they all wanted to see the bag of goodies that I was given.

Mum and Dad were really

proud of me!

How would that make you feel?!

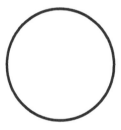

A Few Months Later . . .

So, this was it - I now had the little
baby brother I had always wanted.
I felt confused.

On one hand, I felt so happy,
as I really loved Max.

On the other hand, it was hard

because he cried a lot at night...

sometimes for hours without

stopping!

I don't know where he got all

the puff from!

Mum and Dad were so tired.

They had to get up to feed him and

change his nappy.

Sometimes they were short-tempered and hadn't got time to listen to me, or watch me do things, like they used to.

Sometimes that made me feel a bit lonely, and a bit cross at baby Max. They didn't like ME making lots of noise in case I disturbed Max. But it was OK if Max disturbed ME.

He would scream as I was going to bed, and then scream early in the morning and wake me up.

I was tired at school and Mum had

to explain to my teachers why I was

yawning all the time.

I wasn't bored with their lessons,

or being rude on purpose –

I was just really tired.

How would your face look if you

were as tired as me?

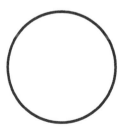

Mum and Dad made sure all my special toys were out of Max's reach so he didn't break anything.

I didn't always like sharing.

I didn't want him to come into my bedroom when I was playing with my building bricks.

I even asked if we could leave Max behind when we went for days out together.

Mum and Dad helped me to see that it wouldn't really be fair on Max. He was too small to look after himself all day.

Do you think my Mum and Dad are right?

Lots of new toys arrived that weren't for me to play with. They came from friends' houses, and some other ones were presents bought especially for Max.

My old toys came out of the loft but Mum and Dad couldn't understand why I still wanted to play with them. They said that I had grown out of them, and that now they were for Max.

I wanted everything Max had.

Sometimes, I didn't really want to play with the cars and the old garage that I had when I was little – but I didn't want Max to play with them either.

It was MY stuff, not HIS.

How do you feel when you're told you need to share?

Lots of people came to the house, and they made lots of fuss of the new baby.

They made a fuss of me too and I was even given a special BIG BROTHER badge but somehow it wasn't the same.

They smiled at Max more than me.

ALSO, Mum and Dad weren't always

there when I wanted them to be.

I had to get dressed on my own,

brush my teeth on my own,

and sometimes play on my own.

They always seemed to be feeding

Max, cuddling Max, changing Max,

bathing Max or just BEING with

Max.

I found it very hard at times.

I didn't understand why I felt angry and frustrated at times. I became louder and fell over all the time, but I didn't know why.

I would slam doors
and shout things like:

"It's just not fair!

You don't care about me

any more!"

or

"It's not the same any

more. You don't have any

time for me!"

Mum and Dad understood though.

They said it was okay to feel like
this. And that I was finding it tough
not being the only child anymore.

They said that older brothers and
sisters often find it difficult having
a new brother or sister.

They explained that Max was more
challenging as he had come
from a difficult place
when we adopted him.

Mum told me that Max's birth
mum and dad loved Max very much,
but they weren't able to look after
him properly. It was thought best
to find another family to
care for him.

I thought it must be hard to be
taken away from your mum and
dad, even if they are having trouble
looking after you.

Dad said
"Max was very poorly before
he came to us. He had been in
hospital a lot as a little baby."

Dad went on to tell me that Max struggled – he had terrible tantrums and would scream really loudly, especially when he did not get his own way. He didn't like being kissed or cuddled and would push everyone away... even me!

How do YOU think Max felt?

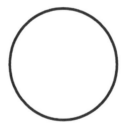

Mum and Dad still got cross with Max and me at times though, even though they were supposed to understand.

I also got cross with Max and would sometimes knock him over or give him a little kick when I thought nobody was looking... but they always were!

I did feel bad doing it, because he was smaller than me, and couldn't kick back. I don't know why I did it.

Mum and Dad tried to spend time with me on my own, away from Max. One of them would take me to the cinema or to the park while the other one stayed with Max.

I also went to my grandparents' house after school one afternoon a week so I could play football with Granddad without Max being there. That was always great fun.

I still wrote in my MAYBE BABY book. It was more private now, and I'd only show people the pages I wanted to, so I could draw or write whatever I like in it, and nobody would tell me off.

I was very proud to be a big brother and I stood up in my class at school and told all my friends about Max.

Mum also came into the classroom when Max was more settled and spoke to the class about adoption.

My friends asked Mum lots of questions.

"What does Max like to eat?"

"What toys does he like playing with?"

"Who said we could have Max?"

"Who is Max's real mummy?"

Mum managed to answer most of the questions... with lots of help from me!

Things began to get easier as Max got older and we all got used to having him in our family.

I liked having him around, and watching him grow up and do new things.

Here and Now!

Max is now 18 months old.

We play ball together.

We play-fight on the floor.

He laughs at me all the time, especially when I am being silly on purpose.

He follows me around and chases me, and I do the same to him.

He gives me big, wet, dribbly kisses, and even wipes his snotty nose on me!

I love playing with Max, he's a brilliant brother!

When my friends come round they sometimes play with Max too. I don't like them playing with him too much because they are still MY friends.

Max sleeps nearly every night now, so that's good.

We've all been on holiday together and I shared a room with Max...and I actually quite liked it!

I sometimes miss Max when I am at school.

I sometimes miss our Social Workers, especially Christine, as they were always interested in me and would always laugh at my jokes and when I fall over on purpose.

Christine gave me a special certificate that I stuck on my bedroom wall.

BIG BROTHER

Mum and Dad still make sure I have my special time with them.

One of them always reads to me every night and I spend some special time with one of them just talking about my day and how I am feeling.

Mum and Dad ALWAYS talk about feelings!

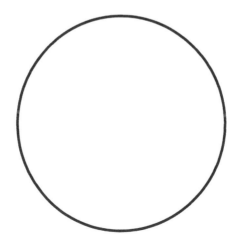

Sometimes my life feels like a rollercoaster of emotions... all up and down! Sometimes they can even make my tummy all jumpy and wobbly.

Getting Max has been a very
long journey.

I have found it difficult to
understand things at times and
frustrated at having to wait.

I have felt sad and angry at times.
I have struggled having to share my
parents, my grandparents, my toys
and my home.

I have felt hurt and confused that I
am not always the centre of
everyone's attention.

I have shown off, played up and
had terrible tantrums.

Through all of this, I have learnt to love and care for my special
little brother.

I have learnt to understand
that sometimes his needs are greater than mine, but also that my needs are important too!

I have accepted him,
just as he has me.

We are brothers.

We are family.

Questions About You...

I have written all about me, so now it's time to write about you.

Getting to talk about yourself and understanding yourself is really important when you are part of a family that is adopting a new brother or sister.

Talk to your parents, they had to write about themselves too.

It might be best to go through these questions with your parents and with your Social Worker. This helps them to have a really good idea of what is going on for you.

Why would YOU like a brother or sister?

How would you feel if your new brother or sister took up all your parents' time?

What is your favourite toy and why? Would you want your new brother or sister to play with it?

What activities do you like to do?
What would you like to do with your
new brother or sister?

What makes you happy?

What makes you feel sad?

How many other different emotions
and feelings can you think of?

If your new brother or sister upsets or hurts you, how would this make you feel and what would you do?

Can you think of different ways to keep yourself calm & relaxed?

When you find things difficult, such as somebody at school being unkind or not understanding your school work, who do you talk to?

Who's involved in the adoption of your new brother or sister?

Write their names here...

Thanks for reading my story — I can't wait to tell you more about me and my brother Max as we grow up together!

Printed in Great Britain
by Amazon